EDGE BOOKS

WORLD WAR II
BY THE NUMBERS

by Amanda Lanser

Consultant:

Cornelius L. Bynum, PhD

Associate Professor of History

Purdue University

Lafayette, Indiana

CAPSTONE PRESS
a capstone imprint

Edge Books are published by Capstone Press,
1710 Roe Crest Drive, North Mankato, Minnesota 56003
www.capstonepub.com

Library of Congress Cataloging-in-Publication Data
Lanser, Amanda.
  World War II by the numbers / by Amanda Lanser.
      pages cm.—(Edge books. America at war by the numbers.)
  Summary: "Describes aspects of World War II using numbers, stats, and
infographics"—Provided by publisher.
  Includes bibliographical references and index.
  ISBN 978-1-4914-4297-5 (library binding)
  ISBN 978-1-4914-4333-0 (eBook PDF)
  1. World War, 1939–1945—Juvenile literature.
  I. Title.
  D743.7.L37 2016
  940.53—dc23   2015000537

Editorial Credits

Arnold Ringstad, editor
Craig Hinton, designer and production specialist

Photo Credits

AP Images: cover (background), 1, 3 (top) 4, 5, 10–11, 13 (all), 14 (background), 15 (left), 16 (bottom), 17 (top, bottom), 20–21, 25,
27 (all), 28–29, Yomiuri Shimbun/Toru Kawashima, 29 (bottom), U.S. Air Force, 3 (right); Corbis: 21, Bettmann, 14 (front), 15 (right);
Flickr: U.S. Army, 3 (left), 12; National Archives and Records Administration, 8–9 (front); Naval History & Heritage Command, 7
(background); Red Line Editorial, 6, 22–23; U.S. Marine Corps History Division, SSgt. W.F. Kleine, cover (front); Shutterstock: aarrows,
7 (ships), admin_design, 17 (Italian flag), Alexandr III, 7 (aircraft), Arkady Mazor, 15 (background), TFoxFoto, 8–9 (background); U.S.
Army, 11 (bottom); U.S. Coast Guard, 2, 18, 19; Wikimedia, 16 (flags), 17 (German Reich flag, Japanese flag), 28 (flags)

Design Elements

Red Line Editorial (infographics); Shutterstock Images: Ken Schulze (smoke)

Printed in the United States of America in North Mankato, Minnesota.
042015   008823CGF15

Table of Contents

MOVING TOWARD WAR

Path to War

1936

January 15: Japan rejects **treaty** restrictions on the size of its navy.

35,000 TONS
maximum **displacement** of warships under the naval treaty Japan rejected

March 7: German dictator Adolf Hitler occupies the Rhineland region of Germany. The move violates treaties signed at the end of World War I that limited his nation's territory.

22,000
troops Hitler sent into the Rhineland

treaty—an agreement between two or more countries
displacement—the weight of the water a ship pushes out of the way; displacement is a way of measuring the size of a ship
Nazi—the National Socialist German Workers' Party, the political group headed by Adolf Hitler
concentration camp—a place where the Nazi regime imprisoned Jews and other persecuted people

After the end of World War I in 1918, few people imagined an even more devastating conflict could be just decades away. But World War II, which began in 1939, was far more destructive. It involved more than 30 countries and caused at least 55 million deaths. Throughout the war Nazi Germany carried out the horror of the Holocaust. The bloody war was the largest and deadliest conflict in the world's history. This is World War II—by the numbers.

1938

November 9–10: A night known as Kristallnacht occurs in Germany; Nazis loot and destroy Jewish shops, homes, and synagogues.

20,000 Jews sent to **concentration camps** by the Nazis in the aftermath of Kristallnacht

1939

August 23: Germany and the Soviet Union sign a peace agreement.

10 YEARS planned duration of the Soviet-German agreement

September 1: Hitler launches an invasion of Poland.

1.5 MILLION German troops used in the invasion of Poland

September 3: The United Kingdom and France, having promised to defend Poland, declare war on Germany. World War II begins.

2 MAJOR ALLIED POWERS AT THE START OF THE WAR: the United Kingdom and France

1 MAJOR AXIS POWER AT THE START OF THE WAR: Germany

THE UNITED STATES ENTERS THE WAR

In September 1940, Japan, Italy, and Germany signed the Tripartite Pact. This agreement linked them together in a military alliance. They became known as the Axis Powers. The United States remained neutral in the war. But tensions between Japan and the United States approached their breaking point in late 1941. The U.S. government did not approve of Japan's aggression toward its neighbors in East Asia. Japan had been building up its ground and naval forces. By November 1941 both countries were preparing for war. Japan struck first. It carried out a surprise attack on the U.S. naval base at Pearl Harbor, Hawaii.

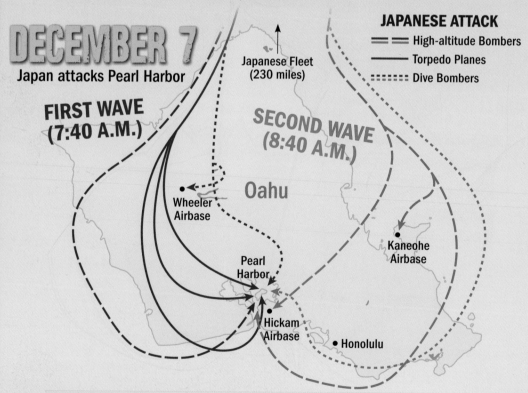

DECEMBER 7
Japan attacks Pearl Harbor

Japanese Fleet
(230 miles)

JAPANESE ATTACK
= = = High-altitude Bombers
——— Torpedo Planes
:::::::: Dive Bombers

**FIRST WAVE
(7:40 A.M.)**

**SECOND WAVE
(8:40 A.M.)**

Oahu

Wheeler
Airbase

Kaneohe
Airbase

Pearl
Harbor

Hickam
Airbase

Honolulu

civilian—a person not enlisted in the military
casualty—a soldier who is dead, wounded, missing, or captured after a battle

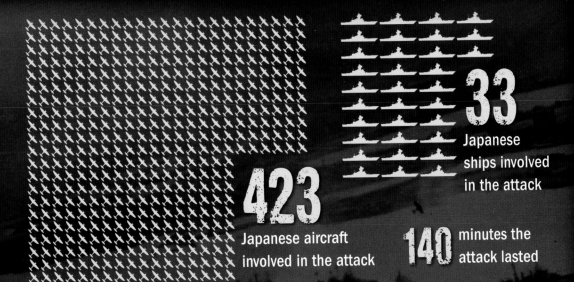

423 Japanese aircraft involved in the attack

33 Japanese ships involved in the attack

140 minutes the attack lasted

86 warships in Pearl Harbor at the time of the attack

American warships lost or severely damaged in the attack **18**

188 American aircraft lost or heavily damaged in the attack

68 American **civilian** deaths from the Pearl Harbor attack

3,478 American **casualties** from the Pearl Harbor attack

1 DAY amount of time between the attack and the U.S. declaration of war on Japan on December 8

DECEMBER 11, 1941 Germany and Italy, Japan's allies, declare war on the United States

AMERICAN FORCES

After Germany and Italy declared war on the United States, the U.S. military was now at war in Europe and the Pacific. U.S. ships began fighting their way across the Pacific Ocean as tanks and troops battled German forces in North Africa in 1942. U.S. troops invaded Italy in 1943 and landed in France in 1944. On opposite sides of the world, they fought against Germany and Japan.

38.8% U.S. troops who were volunteers

61.2% U.S. troops who were **drafted**

250,000 approximate number of U.S. troops sent to Europe each month in 1944

Average Monthly Pay

- $71.33 enlisted soldiers
- $203.50 officers

$0 $50 $100 $150 $200 $250

U.S. Military Personnel

15 million
12 million
9 million — ● Total U.S. Troops
6 million
3 million
334,473
0

458,365
1,801,101
3,915,912
9,623,468
11,623,468
12,209,238

1939 1940 1941 1942 1943 1944 1945

33 MONTHS average length of service for U.S. military personnel

11 major Nazi concentration camps **liberated** by U.S. troops throughout the war

draft—to force to join the military
liberate—to free

9

FIGHTING THE AXIS

JAPAN

The United States had troops and warships ready to strike back against Japan by April 1942. The United States and other Allied countries faced an empire that had grown dramatically in size over the past several years. Spanning mainland Asia, many islands, and a vast area of the Pacific Ocean, Japan was one of history's largest empires. Japan grew its navy in the late 1930s to protect its enormous territory.

2.8 MILLION SQUARE MILES
size of the Empire of Japan in 1942

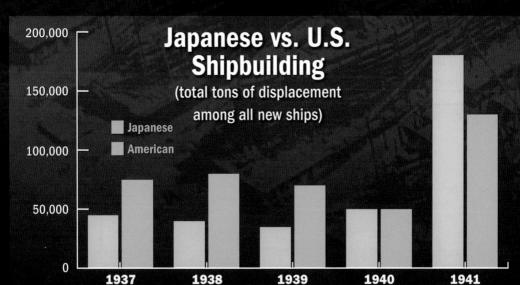

Japanese vs. U.S. Shipbuilding
(total tons of displacement among all new ships)

- Japanese
- American

| | 1937 | 1938 | 1939 | 1940 | 1941 |

GERMANY

By the time the United States entered the war, Germany was in firm control of Western Europe. The Allies needed years to build up an invasion force to retake the continent. In the meantime, they began fighting Germany on other fronts. The first major fighting between American and German troops occurred in North Africa. The large German tanks and their experienced crews defeated U.S. tank forces in their first encounters.

NOVEMBER 8, 1942
the first Allied forces land in Algeria, Africa

FEBRUARY 19-24, 1943
dates of the Battle of Kasserine Pass in Tunisia, the first battle between German and American forces

TANKS DESTROYED IN THE BATTLE OF KASSERINE PASS

183 Tanks

American
German

34 Tanks

0   50   100   150   200

U.S. M3 Lee medium tank

11

WEAPONS OF THE U.S. MILITARY

The United States used a wide array of technologically advanced weapons during World War II. However, more important than these weapons' quality was their quantity. U.S. factories produced weapons in stunning numbers during the war. Unlike Japan and Germany, the United States had manufacturing facilities untouched by enemy bombing. Its efficient production made it possible for the Allies to overwhelm the Axis powers by the war's end.

U.S. Ground Weapons

Weapon	Length	Weight	Ammunition	Effective Range
M1 GARAND RIFLE	43.5 inches	9.5 pounds	.30-caliber bullets	500 yards
M1911 PISTOL	8.25 inches	2.4 pounds	.45-caliber bullets	82 feet
M1917 BROWNING MACHINE GUN	38.5 inches	103.62 pounds	.30-caliber bullets	1,100 yards
M114 155 MM HOWITZER	23.95 feet	6.4 tons	155 mm shells	9 miles

M1 Garand

82 POUNDS
average weight of a typical U.S. soldier's weapons and equipment

P-51 Mustang

U.S. Aircraft

Aircraft	Wingspan	Top Speed	Crew	Range before Refueling
B17 FLYING FORTRESS	103 feet, 9 inches	287 mph	2 pilots, **bombardier**, radio operator, 5 gunners	3,750 miles
P-51 MUSTANG	37 feet	425 mph	1 fighter pilot	1,000 miles

U.S. Ships

Ship	Length	Top Speed	Crew	Range before Refueling
USS *FLETCHER* DESTROYER	376.2 feet	36 knots	273 crewmembers	7,500 miles
USS *MISSOURI* BATTLESHIP	887 feet	28 knots	2,700 crewmembers	14,890 miles

howitzer—a short cannon that shoots shells in a high arc
bombardier—a person who releases bombs on bomber aircraft

THE HOME FRONT AND WORLD WAR II SPIES

The battlefields of World War II were in Europe, Africa, and Asia. But people at home in the United States played critical roles as well. Men and women worked to produce warships, weapons, and other supplies. Families grew their own food and cut their gasoline use to help the war effort. At the same time, however, spies in the United States and in Central and South America worked against the U.S. war effort.

200,000

women who worked in American shipyards during World War II

Home Front

20 MILLION

number of "victory gardens" planted in U.S. backyards between 1941 and 1943. These gardens helped provide food for individual families, freeing up other food sources for the war effort.

2

victories sought by African-Americans under the "Double V" campaign, launched in 1942:
· victory over America's wartime foes
· victory over racism at home

8802 the number of the executive order signed by President Franklin D. Roosevelt banning racial discrimination in America's wartime industries

Axis spy radio

Spies

887 Axis spies U.S. forces discovered in Central and South America between 1938 and 1945

8 German **saboteurs** who landed in the United States in June 1942

40 Axis spy radios the U.S. government **confiscated** in Central and South America during World War II

5 letters from Japanese spies that used the word "dolls" as code for "U.S. warships"

6 number of these saboteurs who were then caught and executed

saboteur—a person who attempts to damage or destroy an enemy's weapons or infrastructure
confiscate—to take property away

WORLD WAR II LEADERS BY THE 3S

3RD presidential term Roosevelt was serving
when the United States entered World War II

Big 3 nickname given to the leaders
of the major Allied countries

Joseph Stalin
Soviet Union

Franklin Roosevelt
United States

Winston Churchill
United Kingdom

1943 Soviet forces defeat
German troops at
Stalingrad, a city
named for Stalin

SEPTEMBER 3, 1939
Winston Churchill takes office
as First Lord of the Admiralty

3

number of major
Axis leaders

Adolf Hitler
Germany

Benito Mussolini
Italy

3RD REICH
Hitler's name for his
new Nazi empire

1943
year Mussolini
was overthrown
and imprisoned

Hirohito
Japan

63
years Hirohito
ruled as emperor
of Japan

D-DAY

On June 6, 1944, Allied forces launched an invasion along the northern coast of France. The area had been under German control since the spring of 1940. The day of the invasion became known as D-Day. It was the first step in pushing the German military out of France.

3 beaches landed on by British and Canadian troops

2 beaches landed on by U.S. troops (code-named Omaha and Utah)

13,000 Allied **paratroopers** who landed behind enemy lines on D-Day

paratrooper—a soldier who jumps out of airplanes with a parachute

4,000–9,000
estimated number of German troops
wounded or killed in the D-Day invasion

10,000
Allied troops wounded
in the D-Day invasion

2,500
Allied troops killed in
the D-Day invasion

50,000 ships, landing craft, and
other transport vehicles
used in the D-Day invasion

Allied Troops and Vehicles in Normandy

150,000 Allied vehicles that had
landed in Normandy by
the end of June

156,000 Allied troops
involved in the
June 6 invasion

850,000 Allied troops in
Normandy by
the end of June

| 0 | 200,000 | 400,000 | 600,000 | 800,000 | 1,000,000 |

THE BATTLE OF THE BULGE

The situation was looking bleak for the Germans in late 1944. That summer, Allied forces had beaten them back from northern France to the German border. At Hitler's command, the German military made a last-ditch effort to push back Allied forces. It launched a massive attack on the Allied front in Belgium's Ardennes Forest in December. The attack created a bulge in the line of Allied troops. German and Allied forces battled in freezing temperatures for more than a month.

3 number of U.S. Army **divisions** in the area where the Germans attacked

30 number of German divisions that launched the attack

division—a large group of troops

The Battle of the Bulge was the last major German offensive of the war. After the battle, U.S. and British forces pushed toward Germany. At the same time, Soviet troops moved into Germany from the east. The Allies surrounded Hitler in Berlin, Germany's capital, in May 1945. Germany surrendered on May 7. The war in Europe was over, but the war against Japan raged on.

75,000
U.S. casualties in the battle

80,000
German casualties in the battle

1/3 portion of Battle of the Bulge casualties caused by frostbite

43 days the battle lasted (December 16, 1944 to January 28, 1945)

85 length, in miles, of the Allied front along the German, Belgium, and Luxembourg border

ISLAND INVASIONS

Japan

China

Pacific Ocean

BATTLE OF OKINAWA
April 1–
June 22, 1945

82 DAYS
length of Okinawa campaign

2,800
Japanese aircraft lost over the course of the battle

BATTLE OF SAIPAN
June 15–July 9, 1944

3 days in which the U.S. Marines were ordered to take the island

3 weeks it actually took to secure Saipan

BATTLE OF LEYTE GULF, THE PHILIPPINES
October 23–26, 1944

10,500 sailors lost by the Japanese at Leyte Gulf

4 major naval battles that made up the Battle of Leyte Gulf

Major U.S. Victories in the Pacific

Many of the land battles in the Pacific took place on tiny, remote islands. The Japanese had conquered these islands in the early months of the war. The United States fought its way from island to island. Conquered islands were used as bases to stage new attacks closer to the Japanese homeland.

Hawaii (U.S.)

BATTLE OF IWO JIMA
February 19– March 16, 1945

6,800 tons of bombs U.S. planes dropped on the island

28,000 casualties the U.S. Marines suffered while capturing the island

BATTLE OF MIDWAY
June 4-7, 1942

51 torpedo bombers launched by U.S. aircraft carriers

44 U.S. torpedo bombers shot down

4 Japanese aircraft carriers sunk by U.S. aircraft

Pacific Ocean

GUADALCANAL CAMPAIGN
August 1942–February 1943

2,500 SQUARE MILES size of Guadalcanal Island

60,000 U.S. troops landed on the island

31,400 Japanese troops defending the island

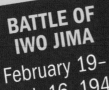

THE HOLOCAUST

Inside Germany and its conquered territories, the Nazi regime carried out one of World War II's most horrific events. Known as the Holocaust, it was a mass killing of Jews and other minority groups between 1933 and 1945. Described by the Nazis as the "Final Solution," the Holocaust involved the murder of Jews, Roma, Poles, Communists, Jehovah's Witnesses, and gay men and women, among other groups.

European Jews

8 MILLION

Jews living in
Europe in 1933

6 MILLION

European Jews
murdered in the
Holocaust

4 MILLION

2 MILLION

0

20,000
total number of forced-labor camps, transit camps, and killing centers built and used by the Nazis between 1933 and 1945

6,000
peak number of Jews gassed to death per day at the Birkenau killing center, part of the Auschwitz concentration camp

12
years Dachau, one of the first concentration camps, operated before its liberation by the United States on April 29, 1945

400
anti-Semitic laws passed by the Nazis in the years leading to World War II

2,711
featureless black slabs that make up the Memorial to the Murdered Jews of Europe in Berlin, Germany

anti-Semitic—against Jewish people

LITTLE BOY

A U.S. B-29 bomber flew toward the Japanese city of Hiroshima on the morning of August 6, 1945. The bomber released its **payload** at 8:15 a.m.: an **atomic** bomb known as Little Boy. The huge explosion emitted a blinding flash of light along with deadly radiation. An enormous blast of air pressure and heat knocked over buildings and started fires. Three days later, a B-29 dropped a second bomb, Fat Man, on the city of Nagasaki. Only a few days later, Japan surrendered. World War II was officially over.

4 years it took the United States to develop atomic bombs (1941–1945)

140 pounds of uranium nuclear fuel used in the Little Boy bomb

15,000 power of the Little Boy bomb, in pounds of normal explosives

payload-equipment or weapons carried by an aircraft
atomic-using the energy created by splitting atoms apart

AND FAT MAN

13.6 pounds of plutonium nuclear fuel used in the Fat Man bomb

21,000 power of the Fat Man bomb, in pounds of normal explosives

120,000 Japanese civilian casualties from the two atomic bombs

5 days after the bomb was dropped on Nagasaki that Japan announced its surrender on August 14, 1945

SEPTEMBER 2, 1945
date of Japan's formal surrender ceremony

AFTERMATH

Troops Who Died

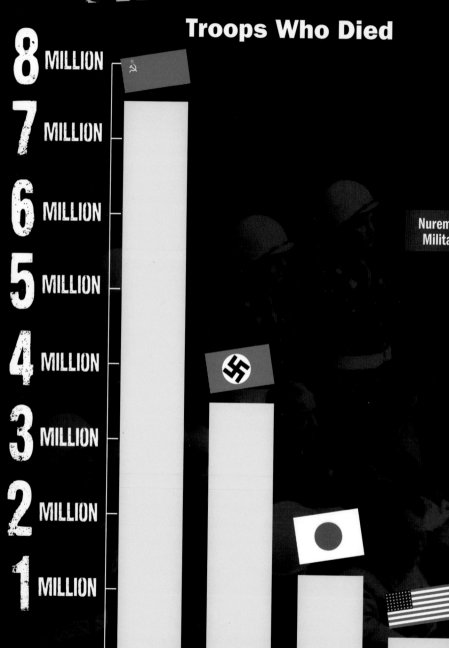

8 MILLION
7 MILLION
6 MILLION
5 MILLION
4 MILLION
3 MILLION
2 MILLION
1 MILLION

Soviet Union | Germany | Japan | United States | United Kingdom

Nuremberg International Military Tribunal, 1946

21 MILLION
number of homeless people in Europe after the war, including people Germany had forced into labor

$12.5 BILLION
cost of the U.S. Marshall Plan, a policy of providing financial aid to European countries after World War II

464
Medals of Honor, the highest U.S. military honor, awarded to U.S. troops for actions during the war

10
high-ranking Nazi officials executed on October 16, 1946, following their sentencing by the International Military Tribunal

MARCH 19, 1975
date the final Japanese soldier surrendered. He had survived for decades in the jungles of the Philippines, not believing the war had ended.

INDEX

TITLES IN THIS SET:

The American
Revolution
BY THE **NUMBERS**

THE
CIVIL WAR
BY THE **NUMBERS**

WORLD
WAR I
BY THE **NUMBERS**

WORLD
WAR II
BY THE **NUMBERS**